BEGINNING **SOLO** GUITAR **First Jazz Standards**

ISBN 978-1-4803-1283-8

7777 W. BLUEMOUND RD. P.O. BOX 13819 MILWAUKEE, WI 53213

Visit Hal Leonard Online at
www.halleonard.com

GUITAR NOTATION LEGEND

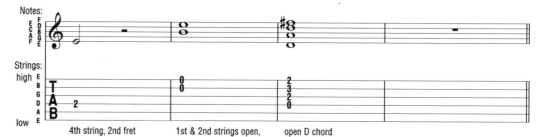

THE MUSICAL STAFF shows pitches and rhythms and is divided by bar lines into measures. Pitches are named after the first seven letters of the alphabet.

TABLATURE graphically represents the guitar fingerboard. Each horizontal line represents a string, and each number represents a fret.

4th string, 2nd fret

1st & 2nd strings open, played together

open D chord

HALF-STEP BEND: Strike the note and bend up 1/2 step.

WHOLE-STEP BEND: Strike the note and bend up one step.

GRACE NOTE BEND: Strike the note and immediately bend up as indicated.

SLIGHT (MICROTONE) BEND: Strike the note and bend up 1/4 step.

BEND AND RELEASE: Strike the note and bend up as indicated, then release back to the original note. Only the first note is struck.

PRE-BEND: Bend the note as indicated, then strike it.

VIBRATO: The string is vibrated by rapidly bending and releasing the note with the fretting hand.

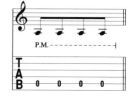

PALM MUTING: The note is partially muted by the pick hand lightly touching the string(s) just before the bridge.

HAMMER-ON: Strike the first (lower) note with one finger, then sound the higher note (on the same string) with another finger by fretting it without picking.

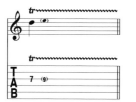

PULL-OFF: Place both fingers on the notes to be sounded. Strike the first note and without picking, pull the finger off to sound the second (lower) note.

LEGATO SLIDE: Strike the first note and then slide the same fret-hand finger up or down to the second note. The second note is not struck.

SHIFT SLIDE: Same as legato slide, except the second note is struck.

TRILL: Very rapidly alternate between the notes indicated by continuously hammering on and pulling off.

TAPPING: Hammer ("tap") the fret indicated with the pick-hand index or middle finger and pull off to the note fretted by the fret hand.

NATURAL HARMONIC: Strike the note while the fret-hand lightly touches the string directly over the fret indicated.

PINCH HARMONIC: The note is fretted normally and a harmonic is produced by adding the edge of the thumb or the tip of the index finger of the pick hand to the normal pick attack.

TREMOLO PICKING: The note is picked as rapidly and continuously as possible.

VIBRATO BAR DIVE AND RETURN: The pitch of the note or chord is dropped a specified number of steps (in rhythm), then returned to the original pitch.

VIBRATO BAR SCOOP: Depress the bar just before striking the note, then quickly release the bar.

VIBRATO BAR DIP: Strike the note and then immediately drop a specified number of steps, then release back to the original pitch.

Additional Musical Definitions

(accent) • Accentuate note (play it louder).

(staccato) • Play the note short.

D.S. al Coda • Go back to the sign (%), then play until the measure marked "*To Coda*," then skip to the section labelled "**Coda**."

D.C. al Fine • Go back to the beginning of the song and play until the measure marked "*Fine*" (end).

Fill • Label used to identify a brief melodic figure which is to be inserted into the arrangement.

N.C. • Harmony is implied.

• Repeat measures between signs.

|1. ||2.

• When a repeated section has different endings, play the first ending only the first time and the second ending only the second time.

All the Things You Are

from VERY WARM FOR MAY

Lyrics by Oscar Hammerstein II
Music by Jerome Kern

Verse
Moderately

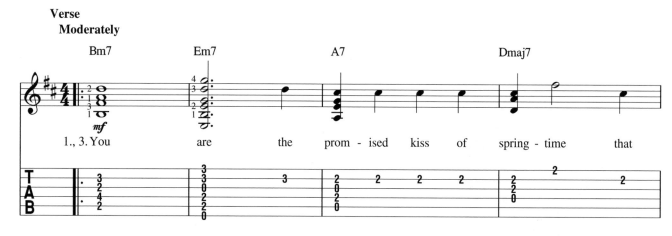

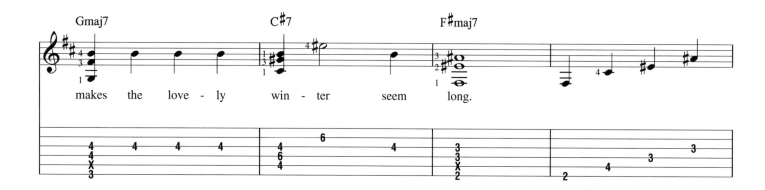

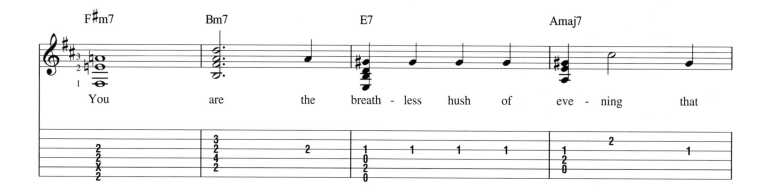

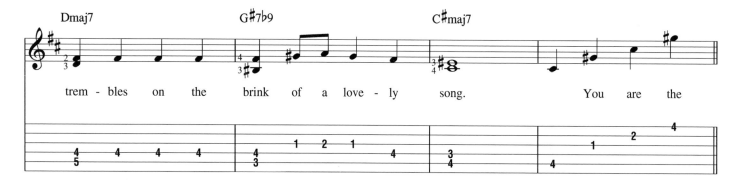

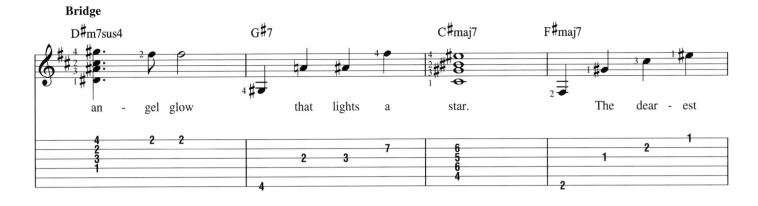

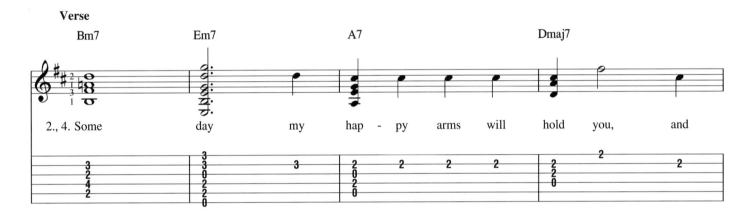

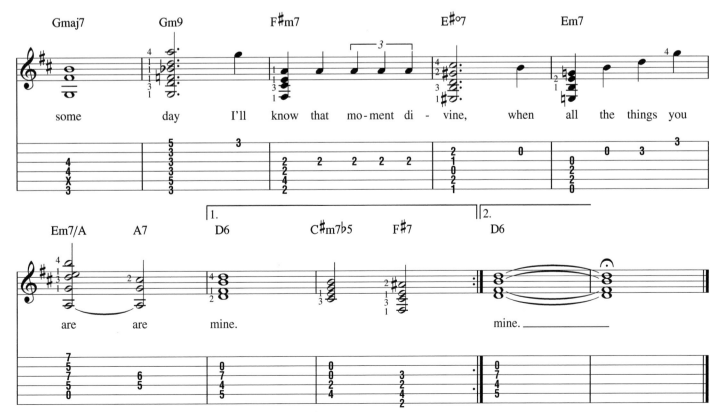

Alone Together

Lyrics by Howard Dietz
Music by Arthur Schwartz

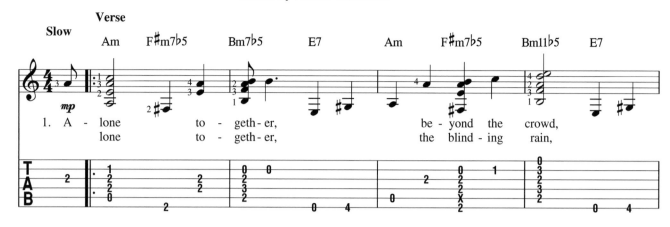

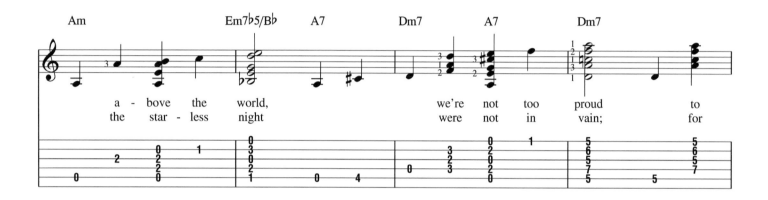

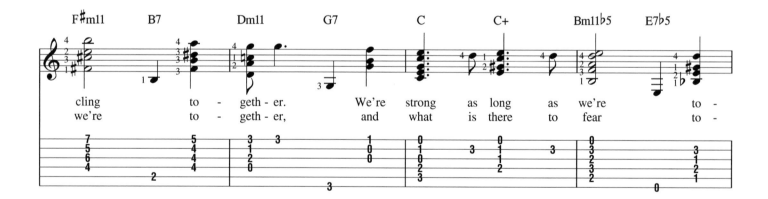

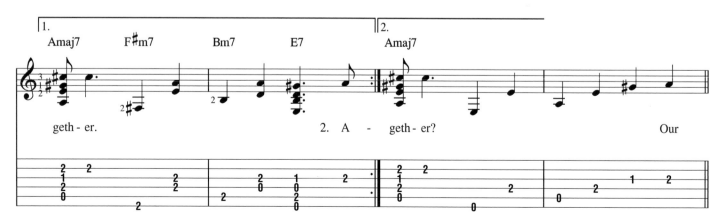

Bridge

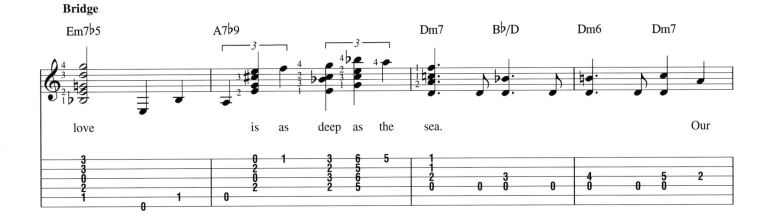

love   is   as   deep   as   the   sea.   Our

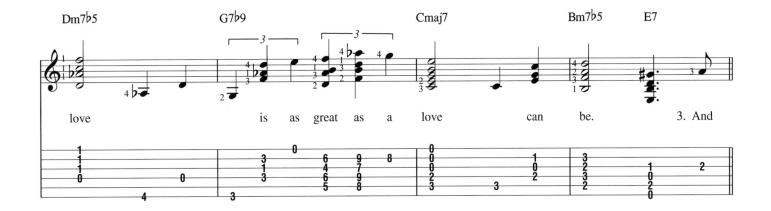

love   is   as   great   as   a   love   can   be.   3. And

Verse

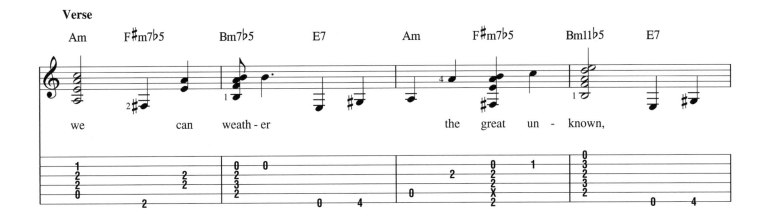

we   can   weath - er   the   great   un - known,

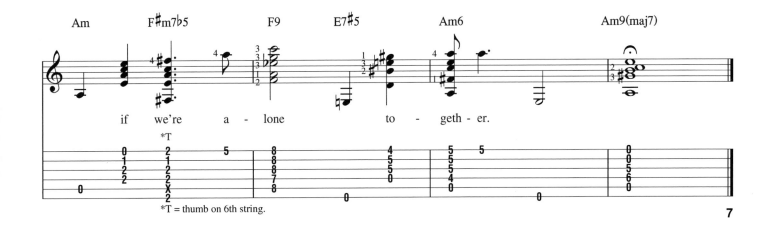

if   we're   a - lone   to - geth - er.

*T

*T = thumb on 6th string.

7

Autumn Leaves

English lyric by Johnny Mercer
French lyric by Jacques Prevert
Music by Joseph Kosma

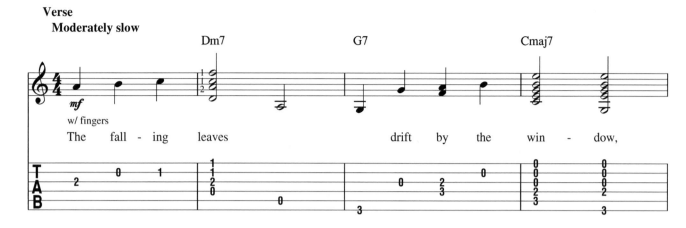

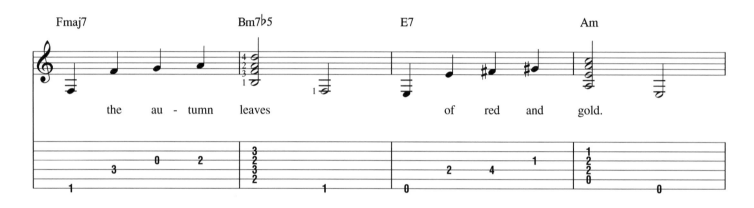

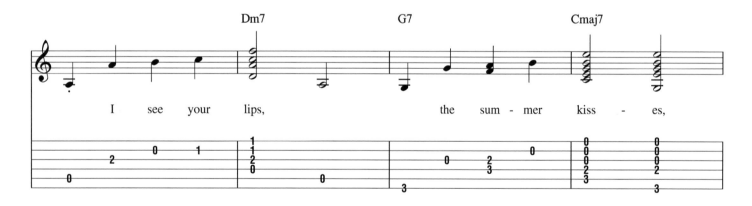

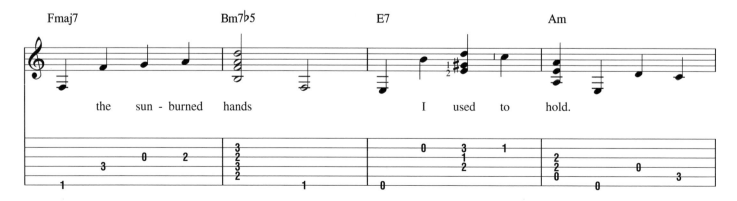

Outro

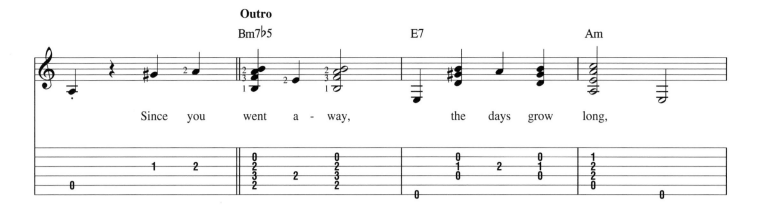

Since you went a - way, the days grow long,

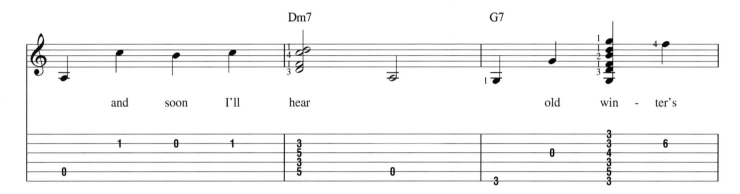

and soon I'll hear old win - ter's

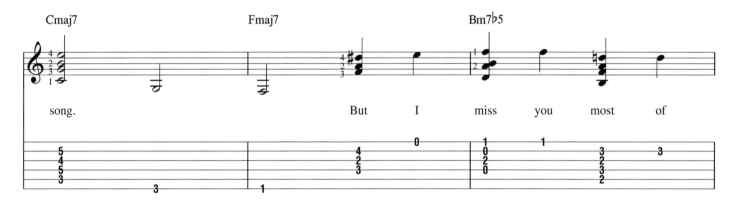

song. But I miss you most of

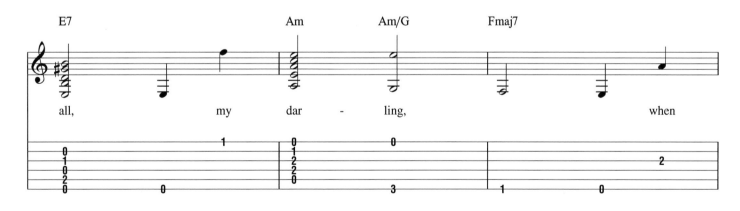

all, my dar - ling, when

au - tumn leaves start to fall. *rit.*

Cheek to Cheek

from the RKO Radio Motion Picture TOP HAT
Words and Music by Irving Berlin

Chorus
Moderately slow

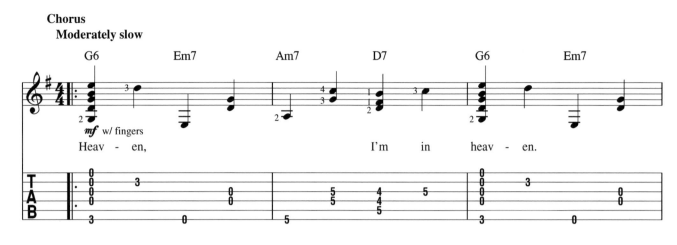

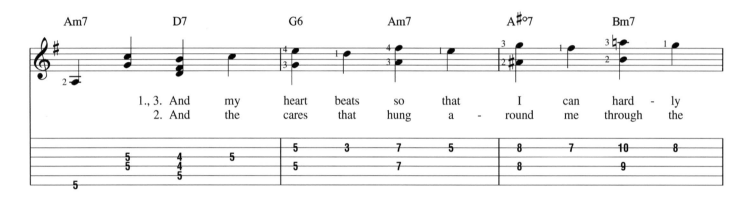

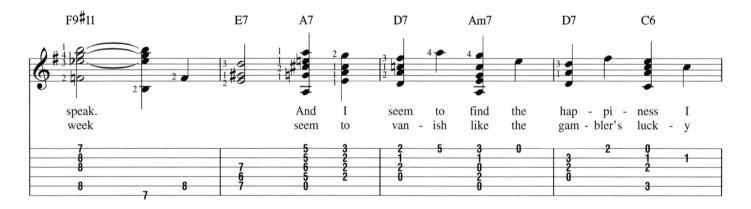

To Coda ✦

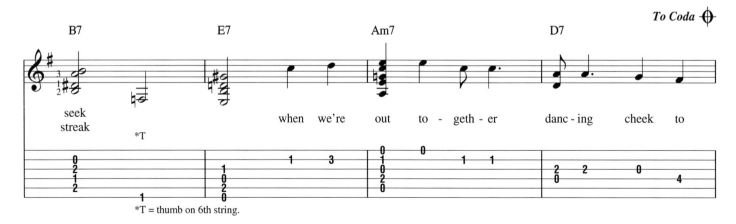

*T = thumb on 6th string.

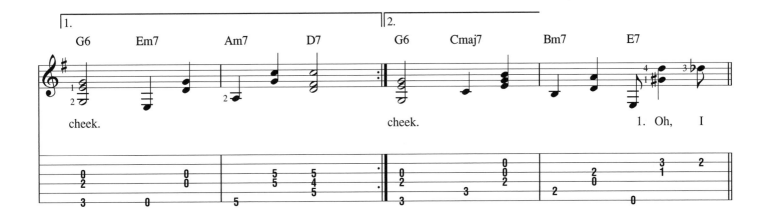

cheek.   cheek.   1. Oh, I

Verse

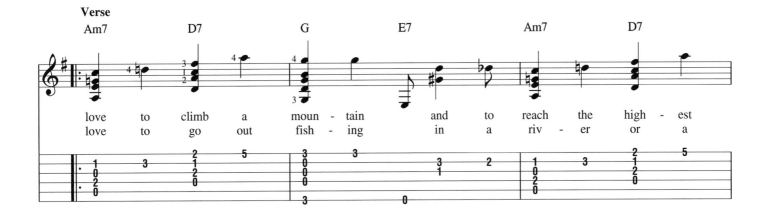

love   to   climb   a   moun - tain   and   to   reach   the   high - est
love   to   go   out   fish - ing   in   a   riv - er   or   a

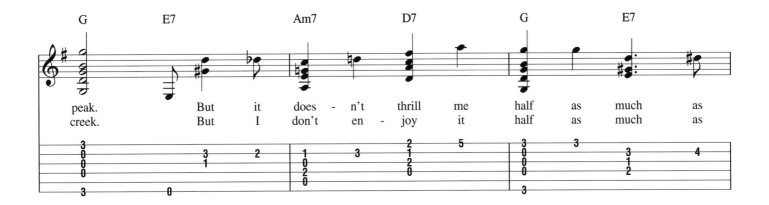

peak.   But   it   does - n't   thrill   me   half   as   much   as
creek.   But   I   don't   en - joy   it   half   as   much   as

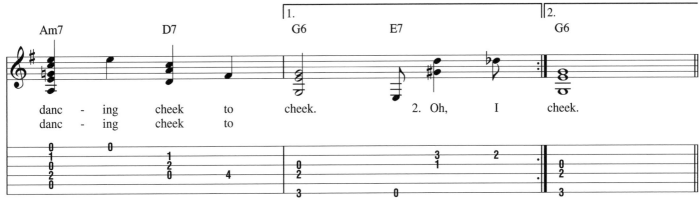

danc - ing   cheek   to   cheek.   2. Oh,   I   cheek.
danc - ing   cheek   to

Bridge

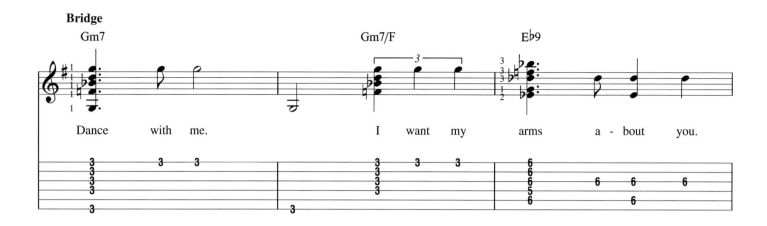

Dance with me. I want my arms a-bout you.

The charm a-bout you will

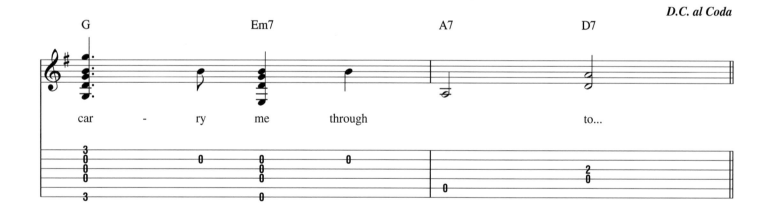

car - ry me through to...

D.C. al Coda

Coda

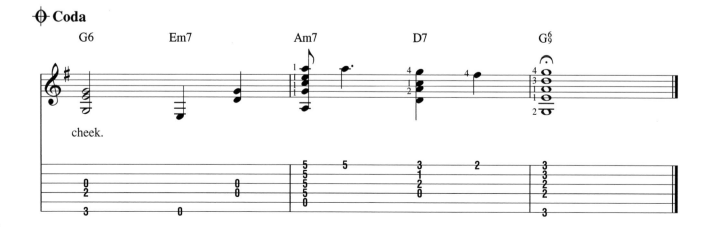

cheek.

Star Eyes

Words by Don Raye
Music by Gene DePaul

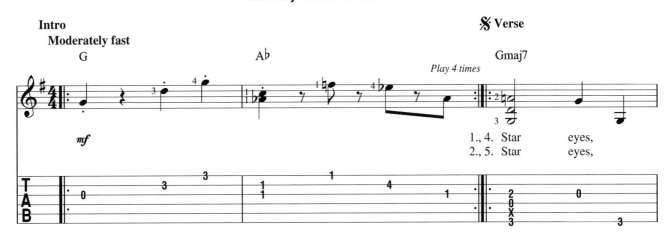

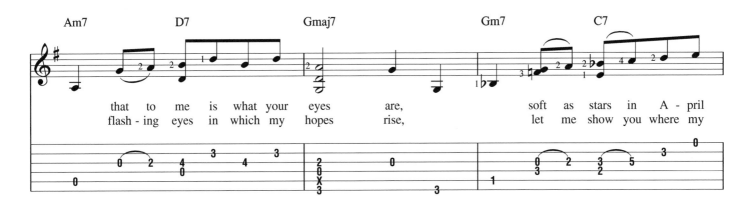

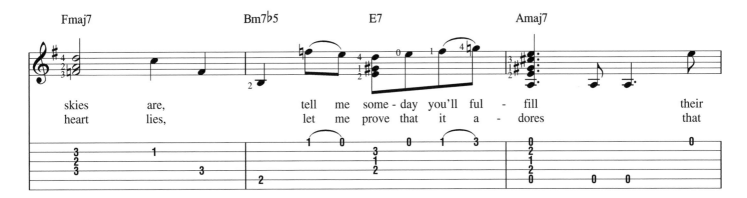

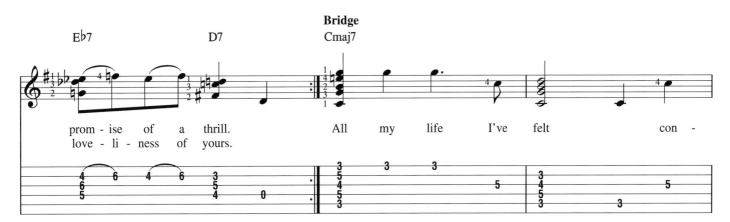

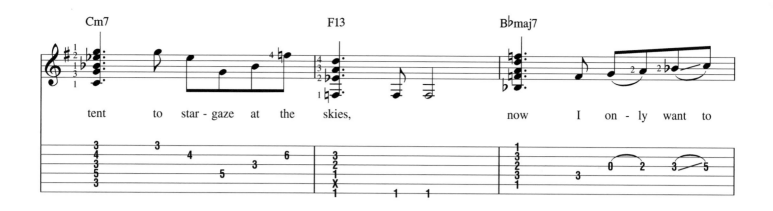

tent   to star - gaze at the skies,   now I on - ly want to

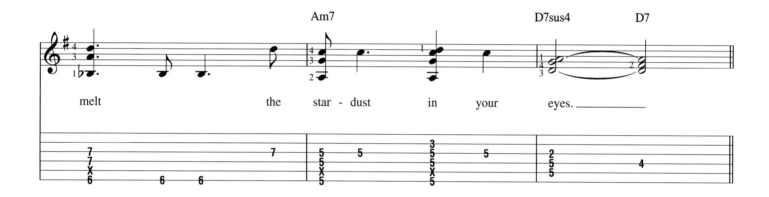

melt   the star - dust in your eyes. _____

Verse

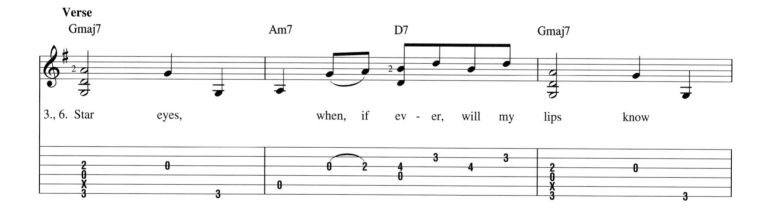

3., 6. Star   eyes,   when, if ev - er, will my lips know

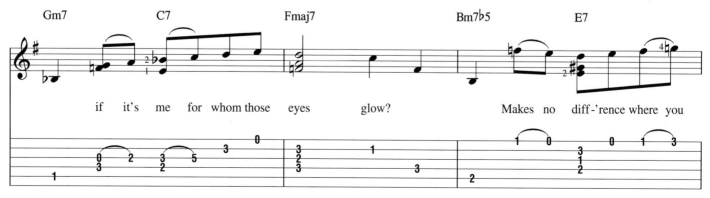

if it's me for whom those eyes   glow?   Makes no diff-'rence where you

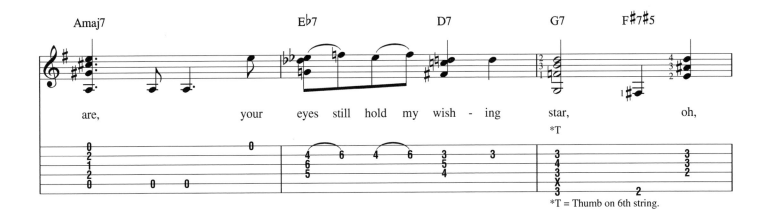

are,   your   eyes still hold my wish - ing   star,   oh,

*T = Thumb on 6th string.

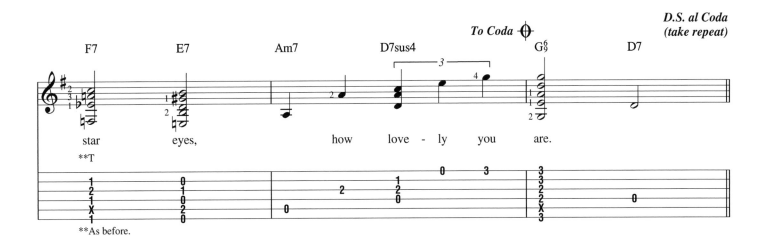

star   eyes,   how   love - ly you   are.

**T

**As before.

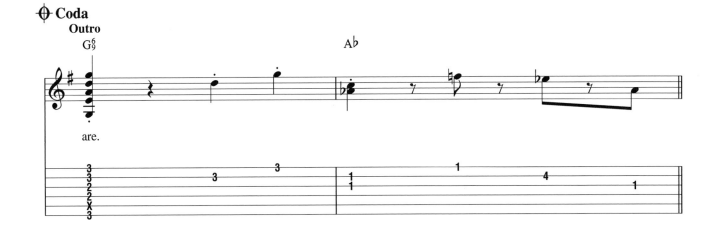

are.

Play 3 times

Don't Get Around Much Anymore

from SOPHISTICATED LADY

Words and Music by Duke Ellington and Bob Russell

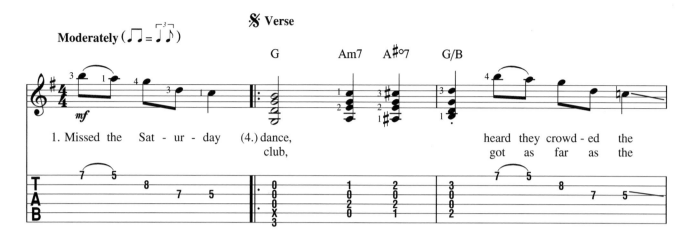

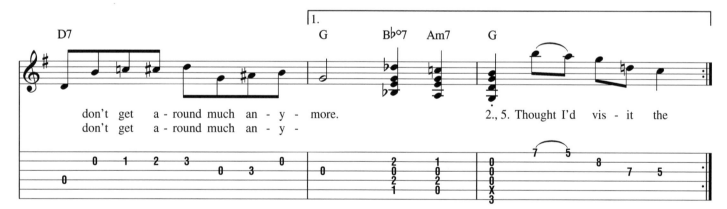

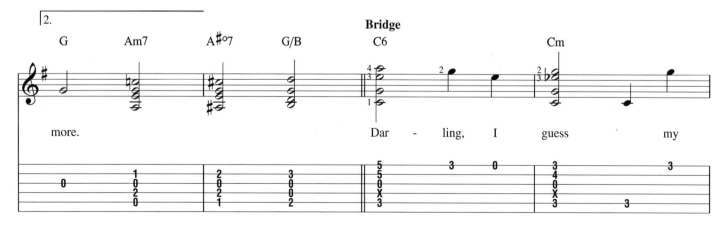

Fly Me to the Moon
(In Other Words)

featured in the Motion Picture ONCE AROUND

Words and Music by Bart Howard

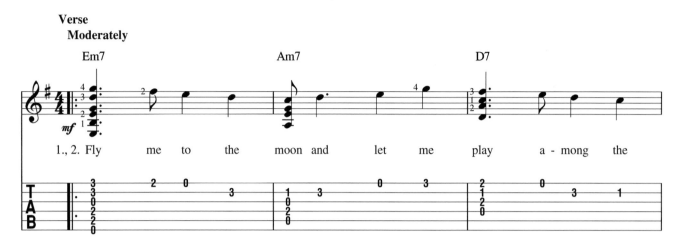

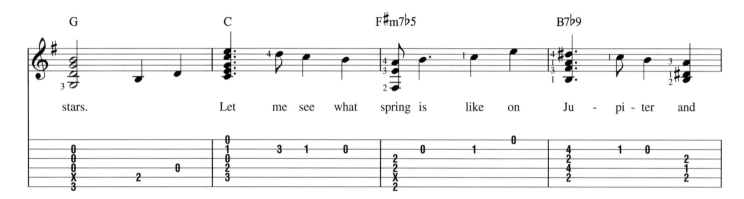

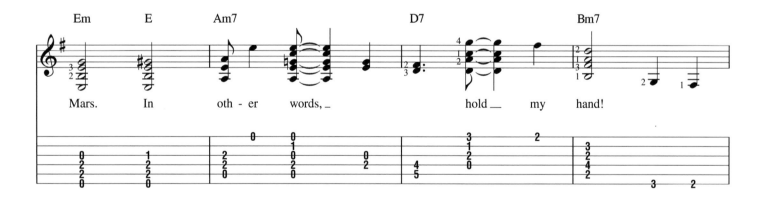

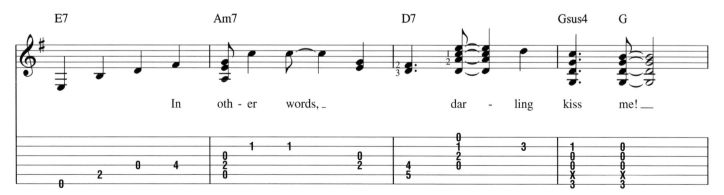

*T = thumb on 6th string.

Georgia on My Mind

Words by Stuart Gorrell
Music by Hoagy Carmichael

Just Friends

Lyrics by Sam M. Lewis
Music by John Klenner

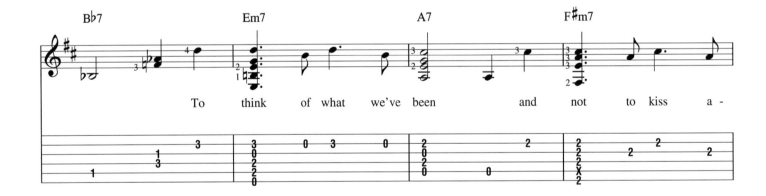

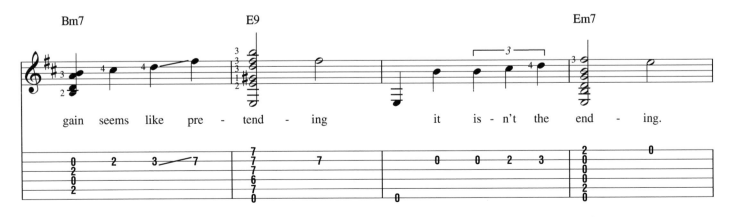

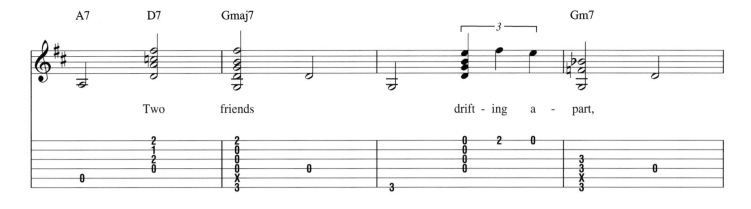

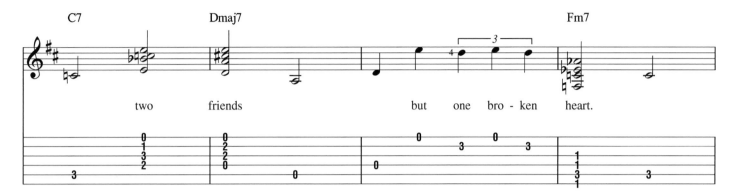

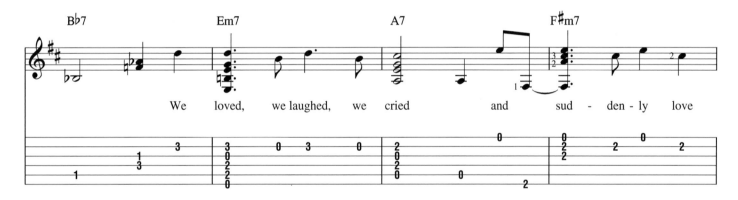

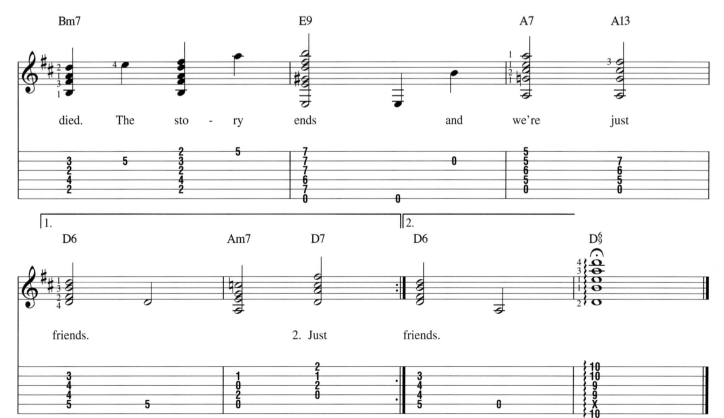

Laura

Lyrics by Johnny Mercer
Music by David Raksin

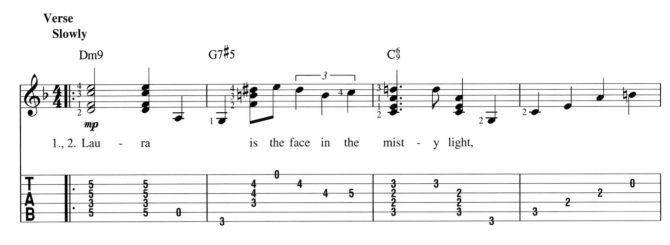

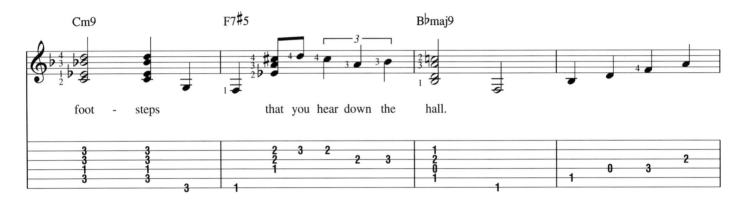

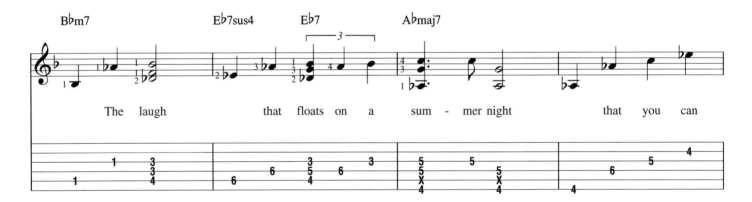

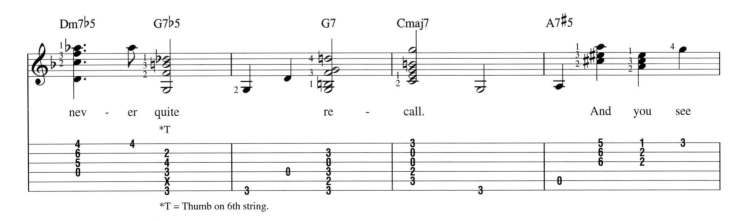

*T = Thumb on 6th string.

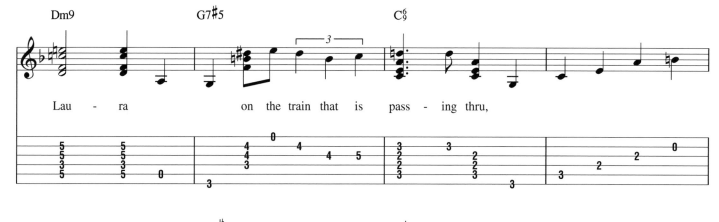

Lau - ra on the train that is pass - ing thru,

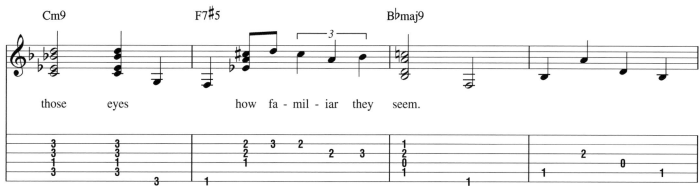

those eyes how fa - mil - iar they seem.

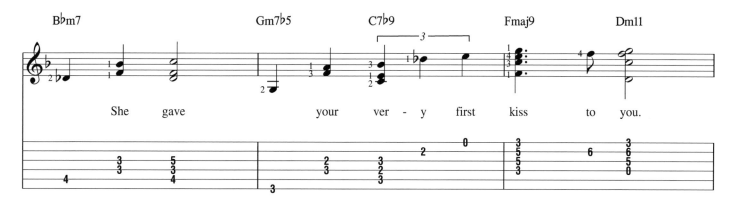

She gave your ver - y first kiss to you.

That was Lau - ra but she's on - ly a

*As before.

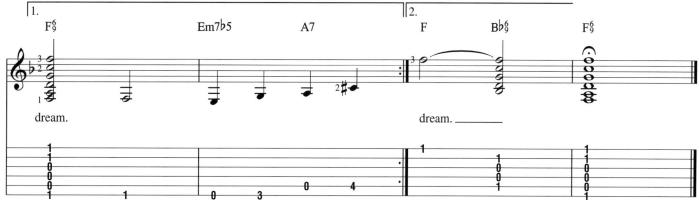

dream.   dream.

Moon River

from the Paramount Picture BREAKFAST AT TIFFANY'S

Words by Johnny Mercer
Music by Henry Mancini

Intro

Moderately slow

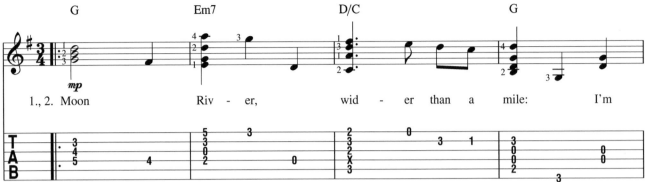
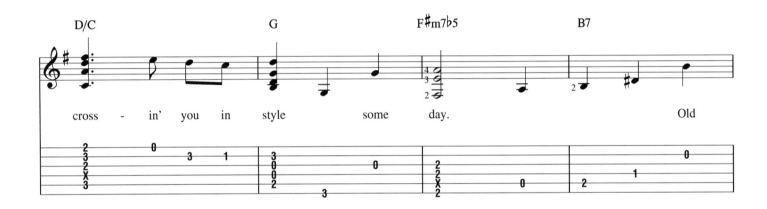

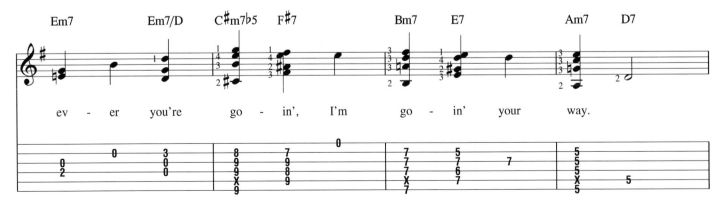

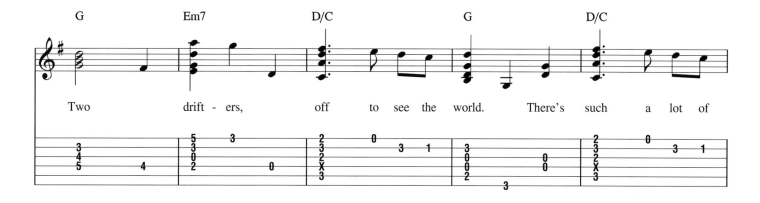

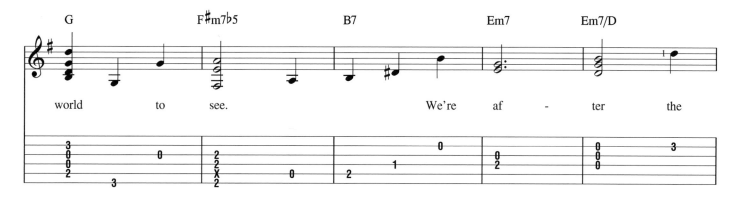

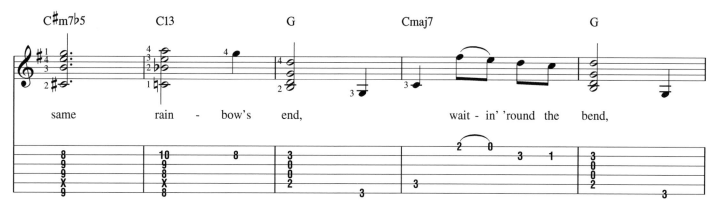

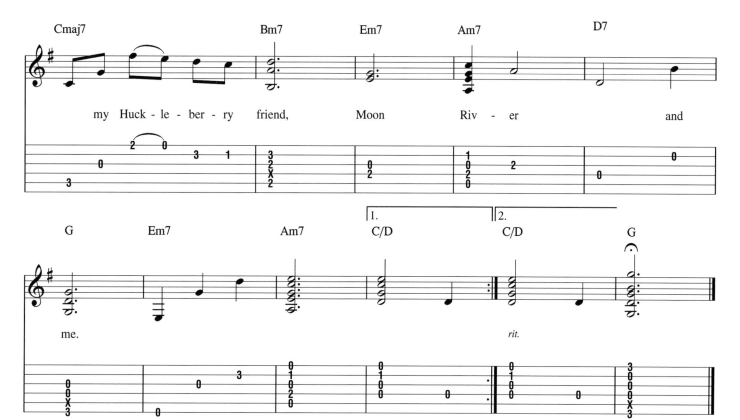

My Funny Valentine

from BABES IN ARMS

Words by Lorenz Hart
Music by Richard Rodgers

Verse
Moderately slow

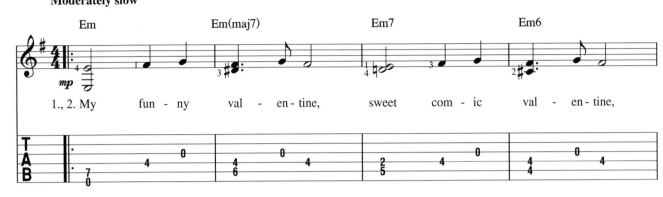

1., 2. My fun - ny val - en - tine, sweet com - ic val - en - tine,

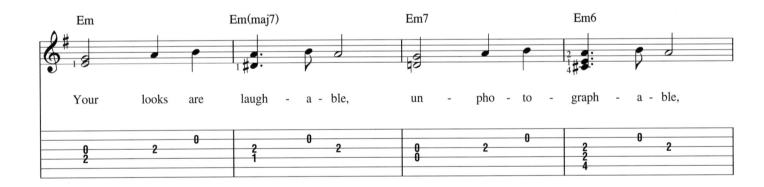

you make me smile with my heart.

Your looks are laugh - a - ble, un - pho - to - graph - a - ble,

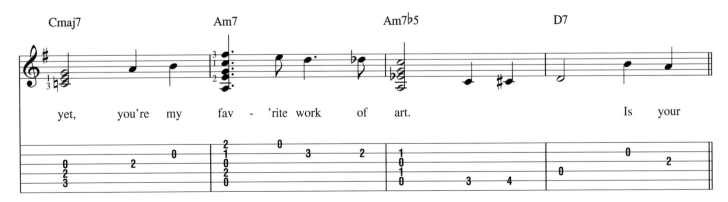

yet, you're my fav - 'rite work of art. Is your

Night and Day

from THE GAY DIVORCE

Words and Music by Cole Porter

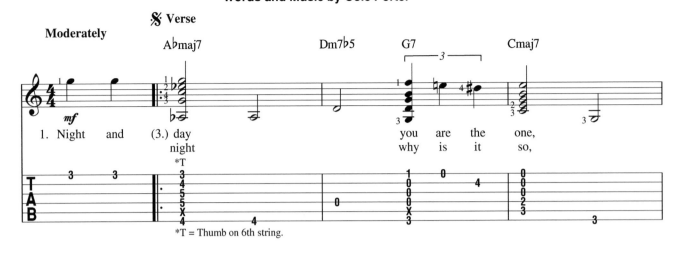

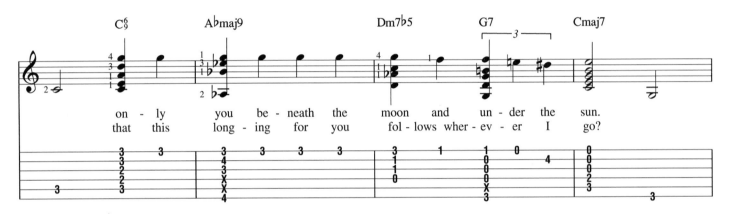

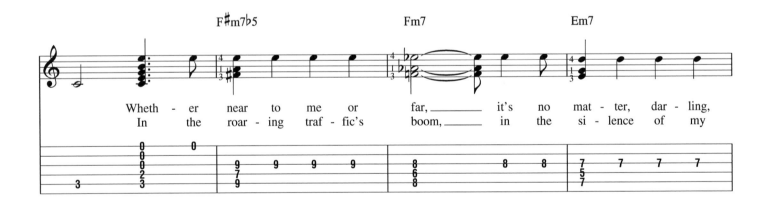

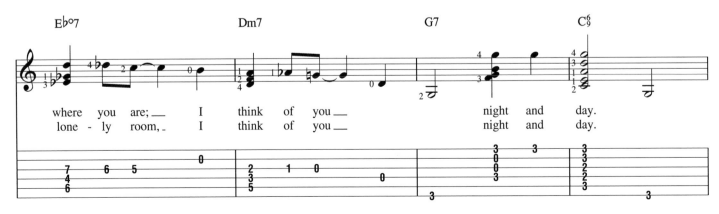

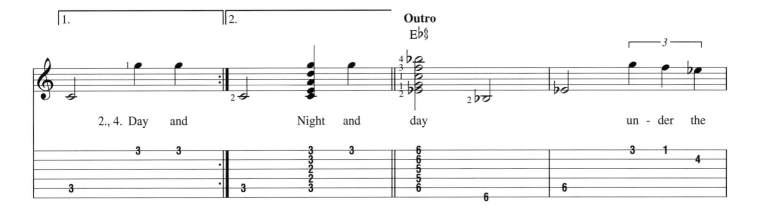

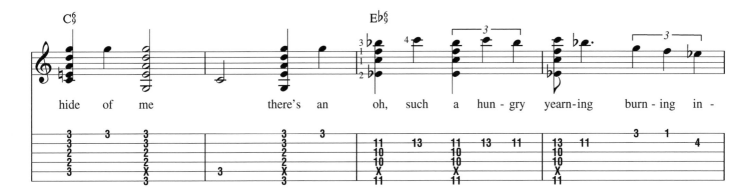

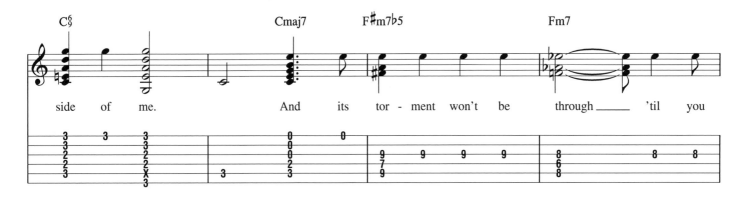

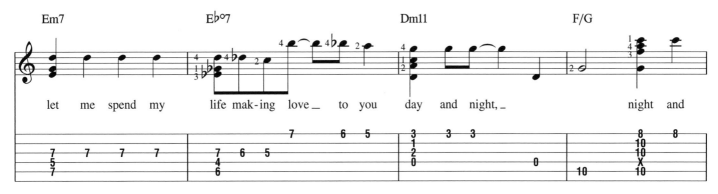

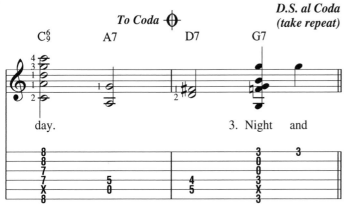

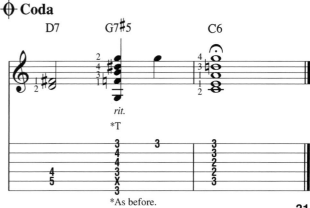

Satin Doll

from SOPHISTICATED LADIES

By Duke Ellington

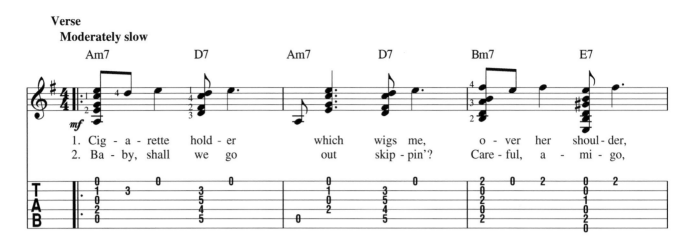

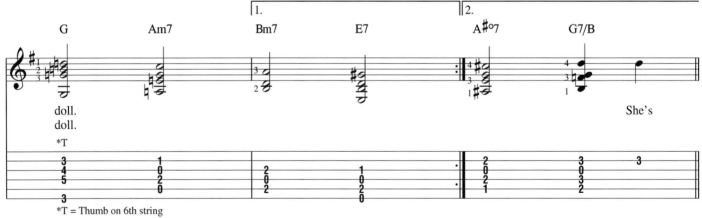

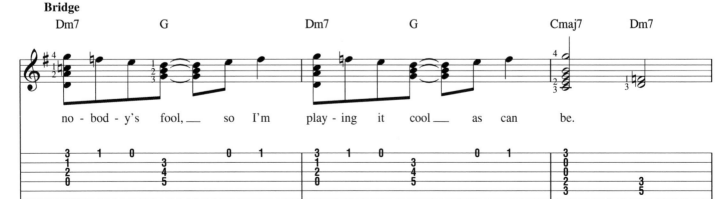

*T = Thumb on 6th string

Summertime

from PORGY AND BESS®

Music and Lyrics by George Gershwin, Du Bose and Dorothy Heyward and Ira Gershwin

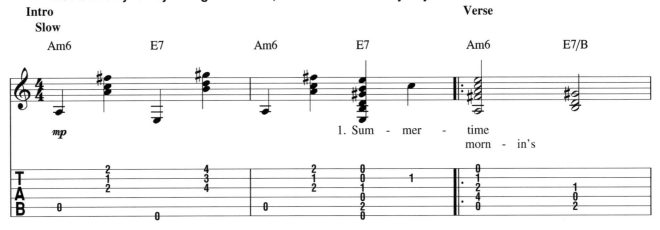

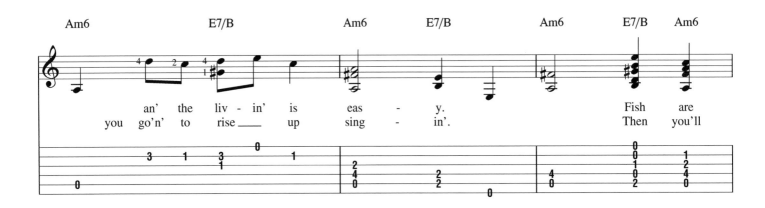

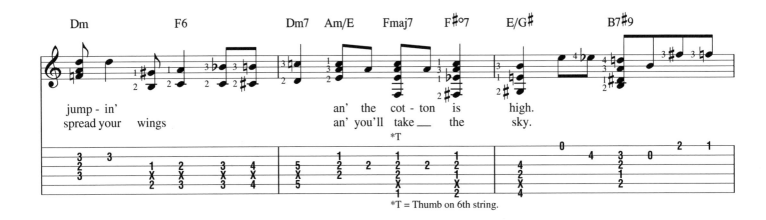

*T = Thumb on 6th string.

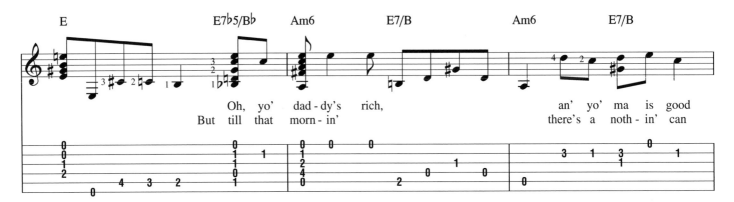

FINGERPICKING GUITAR BOOKS

Hone your fingerpicking skills with these great songbooks featuring solo guitar arrangements in standard notation and tablature. The arrangements in these books are carefully written for intermediate-level guitarists. Each song combines melody and harmony in one superb guitar fingerpicking arrangement. Each book also includes an introduction to basic fingerstyle guitar.

    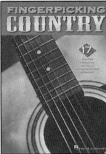 

Fingerpicking Acoustic
00699614 15 songs......................$14.99

Fingerpicking Acoustic Classics
00160211 15 songs......................$16.99

Fingerpicking Acoustic Hits
00160202 15 songs......................$12.99

Fingerpicking Acoustic Rock
00699764 14 songs......................$16.99

Fingerpicking Ballads
00699717 15 songs......................$15.99

Fingerpicking Beatles
00699049 30 songs......................$24.99

Fingerpicking Beethoven
00702390 15 pieces.....................$10.99

Fingerpicking Blues
00701277 15 songs $12.99

**Fingerpicking
Broadway Favorites**
00699843 15 songs......................$9.99

Fingerpicking Broadway Hits
00699838 15 songs......................$7.99

Fingerpicking Campfire
00275964 15 songs......................$14.99

Fingerpicking Celtic Folk
00701148 15 songs......................$12.99

Fingerpicking Children's Songs
00699712 15 songs......................$9.99

Fingerpicking Christian
00701076 15 songs......................$12.99

Fingerpicking Christmas
00699599 20 carols.....................$12.99

**Fingerpicking
Christmas Classics**
00701695 15 songs......................$7.99

Fingerpicking Christmas Songs
00171333 15 songs......................$10.99

Fingerpicking Classical
00699620 15 pieces.....................$10.99

Fingerpicking Country
00699687 17 songs......................$12.99

Fingerpicking Disney
00699711 15 songs......................$17.99

**Fingerpicking
Early Jazz Standards**
00276565 15 songs $12.99

Fingerpicking Duke Ellington
00699845 15 songs......................$9.99

Fingerpicking Enya
00701161 15 songs......................$16.99

Fingerpicking Film Score Music
00160143 15 songs......................$12.99

Fingerpicking Gospel
00701059 15 songs......................$9.99

Fingerpicking Hit Songs
00160195 15 songs......................$12.99

Fingerpicking Hymns
00699688 15 hymns $12.99

Fingerpicking Irish Songs
00701965 15 songs......................$10.99

Fingerpicking Italian Songs
00159778 15 songs......................$12.99

Fingerpicking Jazz Favorites
00699844 15 songs......................$12.99

Fingerpicking Jazz Standards
00699840 15 songs......................$12.99

Fingerpicking Elton John
00237495 15 songs......................$15.99

Fingerpicking Latin Favorites
00699842 15 songs......................$12.99

Fingerpicking Latin Standards
00699837 15 songs......................$17.99

**Fingerpicking
Andrew Lloyd Webber**
00699839 14 songs......................$16.99

Fingerpicking Love Songs
00699841 15 songs......................$14.99

Fingerpicking Love Standards
00699836 15 songs $9.99

Fingerpicking Lullabyes
00701276 16 songs......................$9.99

Fingerpicking Movie Music
00699919 15 songs......................$14.99

Fingerpicking Mozart
00699794 15 pieces.....................$10.99

Fingerpicking Pop
00699615 15 songs......................$14.99

Fingerpicking Popular Hits
00139079 14 songs......................$12.99

Fingerpicking Praise
00699714 15 songs......................$14.99

Fingerpicking Rock
00699716 15 songs......................$14.99

Fingerpicking Standards
00699613 17 songs......................$15.99

Fingerpicking Wedding
00699637 15 songs......................$10.99

Fingerpicking Worship
00700554 15 songs......................$14.99

**Fingerpicking Neil Young –
Greatest Hits**
00700134 16 songs......................$17.99

Fingerpicking Yuletide
00699654 16 songs......................$12.99

HAL•LEONARD®

Order these and more great publications from your
favorite music retailer at
halleonard.com

*Prices, contents and availability
subject to change without notice.*

 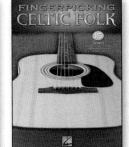   

JAZZ GUITAR CHORD MELODY SOLOS

This series features chord melody arrangements in standard notation and tablature of songs for intermediate guitarists.

ALL-TIME STANDARDS

27 songs, including: All of Me • Bewitched • Come Fly with Me • A Fine Romance • Georgia on My Mind • How High the Moon • I'll Never Smile Again • I've Got You Under My Skin • It's De-Lovely • It's Only a Paper Moon • My Romance • Satin Doll • The Surrey with the Fringe on Top • Yesterdays • and more.
00699757 Solo Guitar............................$16.99

IRVING BERLIN

27 songs, including: Alexander's Ragtime Band • Always • Blue Skies • Cheek to Cheek • Easter Parade • Happy Holiday • Heat Wave • How Deep Is the Ocean • Puttin' On the Ritz • Remember • They Say It's Wonderful • What'll I Do? • White Christmas • and more.
00700637 Solo Guitar............................$14.99

CHRISTMAS CAROLS

26 songs, including: Auld Lang Syne • Away in a Manger • Deck the Hall • God Rest Ye Merry, Gentlemen • Good King Wenceslas • Here We Come A-Wassailing • It Came upon the Midnight Clear • Joy to the World • O Holy Night • O Little Town of Bethlehem • Silent Night • Toyland • We Three Kings of Orient Are • and more.
00701697 Solo Guitar............................$14.99

CHRISTMAS JAZZ

21 songs, including Auld Lang Syne • Baby, It's Cold Outside • Cool Yule • Have Yourself a Merry Little Christmas • I've Got My Love to Keep Me Warm • Mary, Did You Know? • Santa Baby • Sleigh Ride • White Christmas • Winter Wonderland • and more.
00171334 Solo Guitar............................$15.99

DISNEY SONGS

27 songs, including: Beauty and the Beast • Can You Feel the Love Tonight • Candle on the Water • Colors of the Wind • A Dream Is a Wish Your Heart Makes • Heigh-Ho • Some Day My Prince Will Come • Under the Sea • When You Wish upon a Star • A Whole New World (Aladdin's Theme) • Zip-A-Dee-Doo-Dah • and more.
00701902 Solo Guitar............................$14.99

DUKE ELLINGTON

25 songs, including: C-Jam Blues • Caravan • Do Nothin' Till You Hear from Me • Don't Get Around Much Anymore • I Got It Bad and That Ain't Good • I'm Just a Lucky So and So • In a Sentimental Mood • It Don't Mean a Thing (If It Ain't Got That Swing) • Mood Indigo • Perdido • Prelude to a Kiss • Satin Doll • and more.
00700636 Solo Guitar............................$14.99

FAVORITE STANDARDS

27 songs, including: All the Way • Autumn in New York • Blue Skies • Cheek to Cheek • Don't Get Around Much Anymore • How Deep Is the Ocean • I'll Be Seeing You • Isn't It Romantic? • It Could Happen to You • The Lady Is a Tramp • Moon River • Speak Low • Take the "A" Train • Willow Weep for Me • Witchcraft • and more.
00699756 Solo Guitar............................$17.99

JAZZ BALLADS

27 songs, including: Body and Soul • Darn That Dream • Easy to Love (You'd Be So Easy to Love) • Here's That Rainy Day • In a Sentimental Mood • Misty • My Foolish Heart • My Funny Valentine • The Nearness of You • Stella by Starlight • Time After Time • The Way You Look Tonight • When Sunny Gets Blue • and more.
00699755 Solo Guitar............................$16.99

LATIN STANDARDS

27 Latin favorites, including: Água De Beber (Water to Drink) • Desafinado • The Girl from Ipanema • How Insensitive (Insensatez) • Little Boat • Meditation • One Note Samba (Samba De Uma Nota So) • Poinciana • Quiet Nights of Quiet Stars • Samba De Orfeu • So Nice (Summer Samba) • Wave • and more.
00699754 Solo Guitar............................$16.99

Order online at **halleonard.com**

PLAY THE CLASSICS

JAZZ FOLIOS FOR GUITARISTS

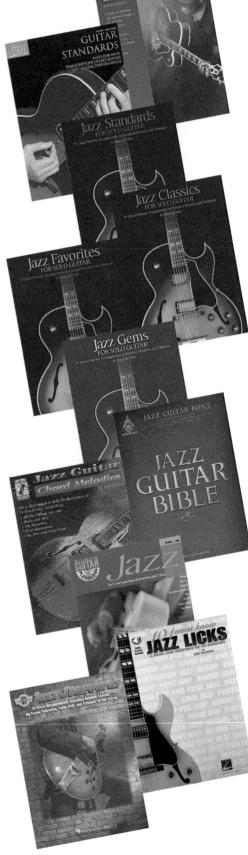

BEST OF JAZZ GUITAR
by Wolf Marshall • Signature Licks

In this book/audio pack, Wolf Marshall provides a hands-on analysis of 10 of the most frequently played tunes in the jazz genre, as played by the leading guitarists of all time. Features: All the Things You Are • How Insensitive • I'll Remember April • So What • Yesterdays • and more.
00695586 Book/Online Audio.................................$29.99

GUITAR STANDARDS
Classic Jazz Masters Series

16 classic jazz guitar performances transcribed note for note with tablature: All of You (Kenny Burrell) • Easter Parade (Herb Ellis) • I'll Remember April (Grant Green) • Lover Man (Django Reinhardt) • Song for My Father (George Benson) • The Way You Look Tonight (Wes Montgomery) • and more. Includes a discography.
00699143 Guitar Transcriptions $14.95

JAZZ CLASSICS FOR SOLO GUITAR
arranged by Robert B. Yelin

This collection includes excellent chord melody arrangements in standard notation and tablature for 35 all-time jazz favorites: April in Paris • Cry Me a River • Day by Day • God Bless' the Child • It Might as Well Be Spring • Lover • My Romance • Nuages • Satin Doll • Tenderly • Unchained Melody • Wave • and more!
00699279 Solo Guitar..$19.99

JAZZ FAVORITES FOR SOLO GUITAR
arranged by Robert B. Yelin

This fantastic 35-song collection includes lush chord melody arrangements in standard notation and tab: Autumn in New York • Call Me Irresponsible • How Deep Is the Ocean • I Could Write a Book • The Lady Is a Tramp • Mood Indigo • Polka Dots and Moonbeams • Solitude • Take the "A" Train • Where or When • more.
00699278 Solo Guitar $19.99

JAZZ GEMS FOR SOLO GUITAR
arranged by Robert B. Yelin

35 great solo arrangements of jazz classics, including: After You've Gone • Alice in Wonderland • The Christmas Song • Four • Meditation • Stompin' at the Savoy • Sweet and Lovely • Waltz for Debby • Yardbird Suite • You'll Never Walk Alone • You've Changed • and more.
00699617 Solo Guitar $19.99

JAZZ GUITAR BIBLE

The one book that has all of the jazz guitar classics transcribed note-for-note, with standard notation and tablature. Includes over 30 songs: Body and Soul • Girl Talk • I'll Remember April • In a Sentimental Mood • My Funny Valentine • Nuages • Satin Doll • So What • Stardust • Take Five • Tangerine • Yardbird Suite • and more.
00690466 Guitar Recorded Versions $27.99

JAZZ GUITAR CHORD MELODIES
arranged & performed by Dan Towey

This book/CD pack includes complete solo performances of 12 standards, including: All the Things You Are • Body and Soul • My Romance • How Insensitive • My One and Only Love • and more. The arrangements are performance level and range in difficulty from intermediate to advanced.
00698988 Book/CD Pack.......................................$19.95

JAZZ GUITAR PLAY-ALONG
Guitar Play-Along Volume 16

With this book/audio pack, all you have to do is follow the tab, listen to the online audio to hear how the guitar should sound, and then play along using the separate backing tracks. 8 songs: All Blues • Bluesette • Footprints • How Insensitive (Insensatez) • Misty • Satin Doll • Stella by Starlight • Tenor Madness.
00699584 Book/Online Audio...............................$16.99

JAZZ STANDARDS FOR FINGERSTYLE GUITAR

20 songs, including: All the Things You Are • Autumn Leaves • Bluesette • Body and Soul • Fly Me to the Moon • The Girl from Ipanema • How Insensitive • I've Grown Accustomed to Her Face • My Funny Valentine • Satin Doll • Stompin' at the Savoy • and more.
00699029 Fingerstyle Guitar $17.99

JAZZ STANDARDS FOR SOLO GUITAR
arranged by Robert B. Yelin

35 chord melody guitar arrangements, including: Ain't Misbehavin' • Autumn Leaves • Bewitched • Cherokee • Darn That Dream • Girl Talk • I've Got You Under My Skin • Lullaby of Birdland • My Funny Valentine • A Nightingale Sang in Berkeley Square • Stella by Starlight • The Very Thought of You • and more.
00699277 Solo Guitar $19.99

101 MUST-KNOW JAZZ LICKS
by Wolf Marshall

Add a jazz feel and flavor to your playing! 101 definitive licks, plus demonstration audio, from every major jazz guitar style, neatly organized into easy-to-use categories. They're all here: swing and pre-bop, bebop, post-bop modern jazz, hard bop and cool jazz, modal jazz, soul jazz and postmodern jazz.
00695433 Book/Online Audio...............................$19.99

HAL•LEONARD®

Visit Hal Leonard Online at **www.halleonard.com**

Prices, contents and availability subject to change without notice.

IMPROVE YOUR IMPROV
AND OTHER JAZZ TECHNIQUES WITH BOOKS FROM HAL LEONARD

JAZZ GUITAR

Hal Leonard Guitar Method
by Jeff Schroedl

The Hal Leonard Jazz Guitar Method is your complete guide to learning jazz guitar. This book uses real jazz songs to teach the basics of accompanying and improvising jazz guitar in the style of Wes Montgomery, Joe Pass, Tal Farlow, Charlie Christian, Pat Martino, Barney Kessel, Jim Hall, and many others.
00695359 Book/Online Audio $22.99

AMAZING PHRASING
50 Ways to Improve Your
Improvisational Skills • *by Tom Kolb*

This book explores all the main components necessary for crafting well-balanced rhythmic and melodic phrases. It also explains how these phrases are put together to form cohesive solos. Many styles are covered – rock, blues, jazz, fusion, country, Latin, funk and more – and all of the concepts are backed up with musical examples.
00695583 Book/Online Audio $22.99

BEST OF JAZZ GUITAR
by Wolf Marshall • Signature Licks

In this book/audio pack, Wolf Marshall provides a hands-on analysis of 10 of the most frequently played tunes in the jazz genre, as played by the leading guitarists of all time. Each selection includes technical analysis and performance notes, biographical sketches, and authentic matching audio with backing tracks.
00695586 Book/Online Audio $29.99

CHORD-MELODY PHRASES FOR GUITAR
by Ron Eschete • REH ProLessons Series

Expand your chord-melody chops with these outstanding jazz phrases! This book covers: chord substitutions, chromatic movements, contrary motion, pedal tones, inner-voice movements, reharmonization techniques, and much more. Includes standard notation and tab, and online audio.
00695628 Book/Online Audio $17.99

CHORDS FOR JAZZ GUITAR
The Complete Guide to Comping,
Chord Melody and Chord Soloing • *by Charlton Johnson*

This book/audio pack will teach you how to play jazz chords all over the fretboard in a variety of styles and progressions. It covers: voicings, progressions, jazz chord theory, comping, chord melody, chord soloing, voice leading and many more topics. The audio offers 98 full-band demo tracks. No tablature.
00695706 Book/Online Audio $19.99

FRETBOARD ROADMAPS – JAZZ GUITAR
The Essential Guitar Patterns
That All the Pros Know and Use • *by Fred Sokolow*

This book will get guitarists playing lead & rhythm anywhere on the fretboard, in any key! It teaches a variety of lead guitar styles using moveable patterns, double-note licks, sliding pentatonics and more, through easy-to-follow diagrams and instructions. The online audio includes 54 full-demo tracks.
00695354 Book/Online Audio $17.99

JAZZ IMPROVISATION FOR GUITAR

by Les Wise • REH ProLessons Series

This book/audio will allow you to make the transition from playing disjointed scales and arpeggios to playing melodic jazz solos that maintain continuity and interest for the listener. Topics covered include: tension and resolution, major scale, melodic minor scale, and harmonic minor scale patterns, common licks and substitution techniques, creating altered tension, and more! Features standard notation and tab, and online audio.
00695657 Book/Online Audio $19.99

JAZZ RHYTHM GUITAR

The Complete Guide
by Jack Grassel

This book/audio pack will help rhythm guitarists better understand: chord symbols and voicings, comping styles and patterns, equipment, accessories and set-up, the fingerboard, chord theory, and much more. The accompanying online audio includes 74 full-band tracks.
00695654 Book/Online Audio $24.99

JAZZ SOLOS FOR GUITAR

Lead Guitar in the Styles of Tal Farlow,
Barney Kessel, Wes Montgomery, Joe Pass, Johnny Smith
by Les Wise

Examine the solo concepts of the masters with this book including phrase-by-phrase performance notes, tips on arpeggio substitution, scale substitution, tension and resolution, jazz-blues, chord soloing, and more. The audio includes full demonstration and rhythm-only tracks.
00695447 Book/Online Audio $19.99

100 JAZZ LESSONS
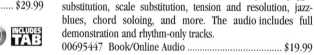
Guitar Lesson Goldmine Series
by John Heussenstamm and Paul Silbergleit

Featuring 100 individual modules covering a giant array of topics, each lesson includes detailed instruction with playing examples presented in standard notation and tablature. You'll also get extremely useful tips, scale diagrams, and more to reinforce your learning experience, plus audio featuring performance demos of all the examples in the book!
00696454 Book/Online Audio $24.99

101 MUST-KNOW JAZZ LICKS

A Quick, Easy Reference Guide
for All Guitarists • *by Wolf Marshall*

Here are 101 definitive licks, plus demonstration audio, from every major jazz guitar style, neatly organized into easy-to-use categories. They're all here: swing and pre-bop, bebop, post-bop modern jazz, hard bop and cool jazz, modal jazz, soul jazz and postmodern jazz. Includes an introduction, tips, and a list of suggested recordings.
00695433 Book/Online Audio $19.99

SWING AND BIG BAND GUITAR

Four-to-the-Bar Comping in the Style of
Freddie Green • *by Charlton Johnson*

This unique package teaches the essentials of swing and big band styles, including chord voicings, inversions, substitutions; time and groove, reading charts, chord reduction, and expansion; sample songs, patterns, progressions, and exercises; chord reference library; and online audio with over 50 full-demo examples. Uses chord grids – no tablature.
00695147 Book/Online Audio $22.99

Visit Hal Leonard Online at **www.halleonard.com**

*Prices, contents and availability
subject to change without notice.*